"To laugh is the music of the soul"

Dedicated to:
Natalie, Stan, Paull,
Jyl, Teresa, Poco,
Bessie and Cookie

With Special Thanks to:
Larry Barnes
Gary Gertzweig
LRH
Judith Mullen

FIRST PRINTING SEPTEMBER 1981
SECOND PRINTING JANUARY 1982
THIRD PRINTING DECEMBER 1982
FOURTH PRINTING OCTOBER 1983

Published by:
Rubes Publications
14447 Titus St.
Panorama City, CA 91402

Notable Quotes/1981

© Copyright 1981 Leigh Rubin

All rights reserved

Library of Congress Catalog Card Number:
81-69508

ISBN: 0-941364-00-3

Book Design by Wong Design
Photography by Lester Cohen

Printed in the United States of America

"So the doctor told me to take two aspirin and stay <u>composed</u>."

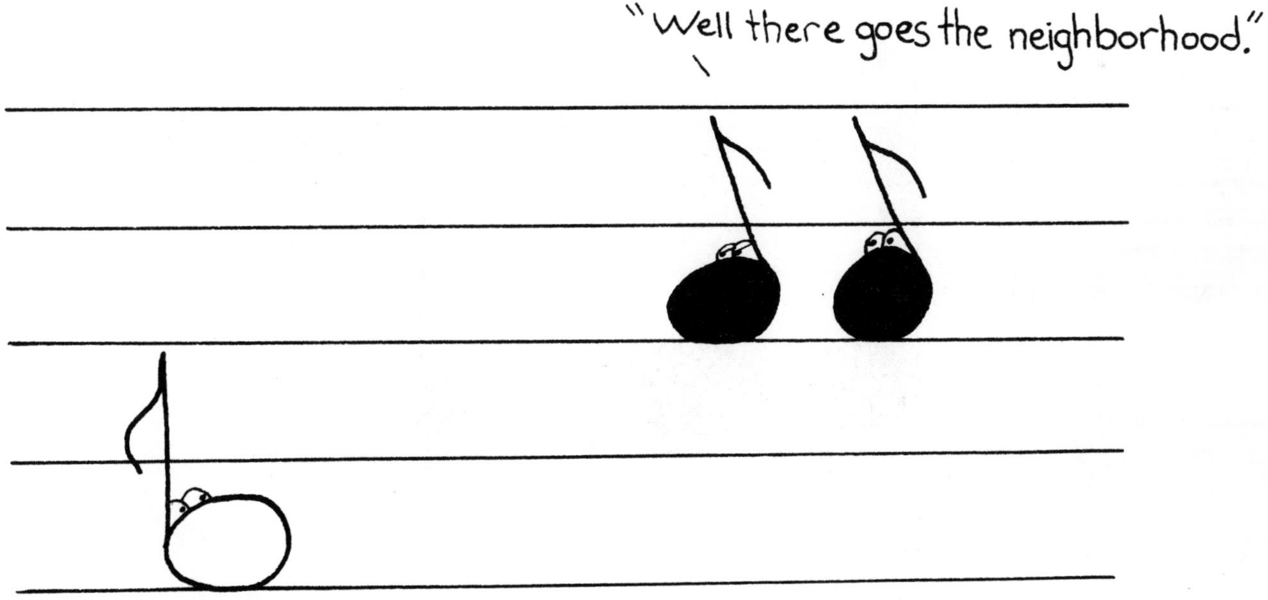
"Well there goes the neighborhood."

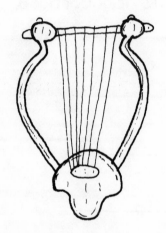

"I don't care what he says, he'll always be a lyre!"

"my wife and my best friend,... how long has this <u>arrangement</u> been going on?"

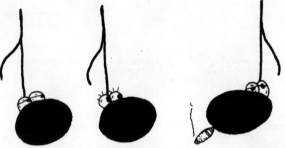

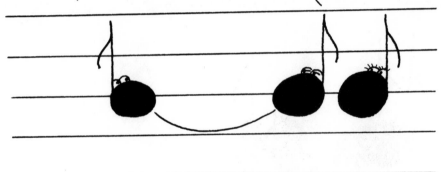

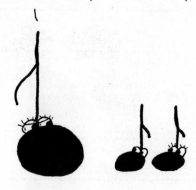

"They're good kids, but I just can't get them to eat their beats."

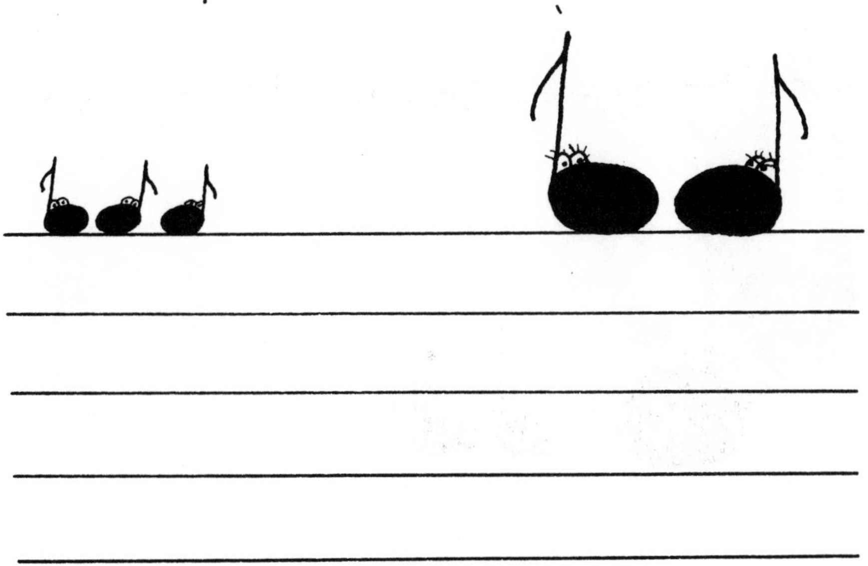

"What was it like before stereo, Gramps?"

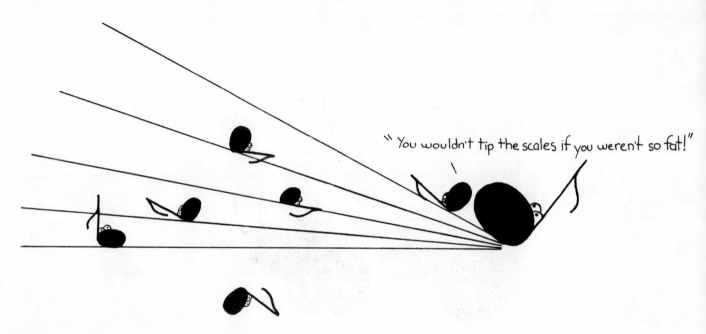

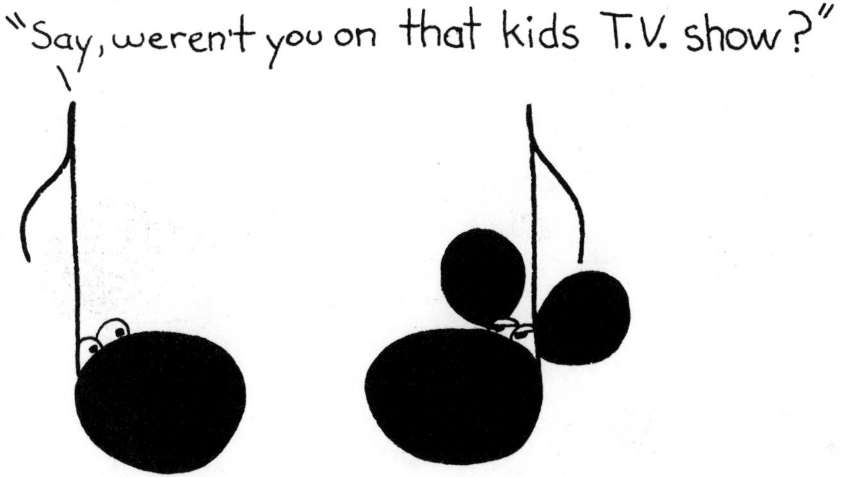
"Say, weren't you on that kids T.V. show?"

"Hey, I saw that guy on the Lawrence Welk show!"

"Sorry, no minors allowed in this bar."

"why don't you get a real job and quit singing the blues."

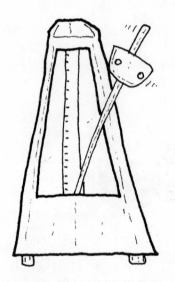

" There's nothing worse than a boss who makes sure you're on time."

"And another thing, any more <u>feedback</u> out of you and you're fired!"

"Now that all the paperwork is done, I'll just need your signature."

"He was big in the '20s but it's another case of riches to ragtime."

"Oldtimer, your bootlegging days are over!"

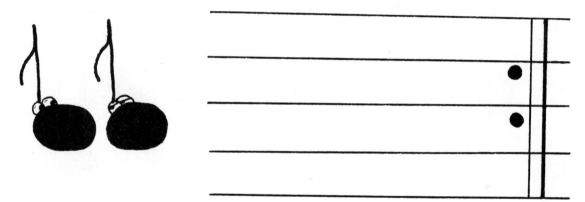

"He may be <u>sharp</u> but he's a showoff."

"I liked her better before she went <u>platinum</u>."

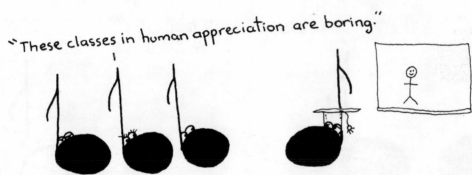

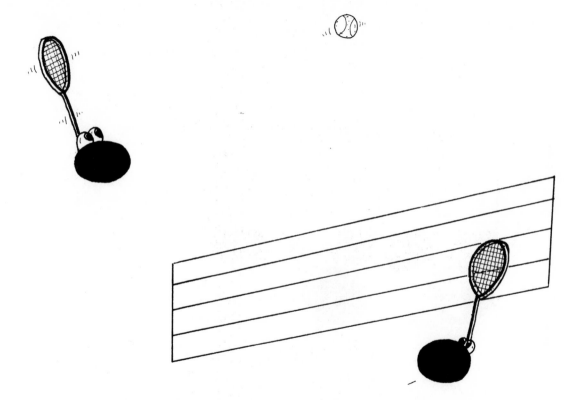

"After such a long set I need a rest!"

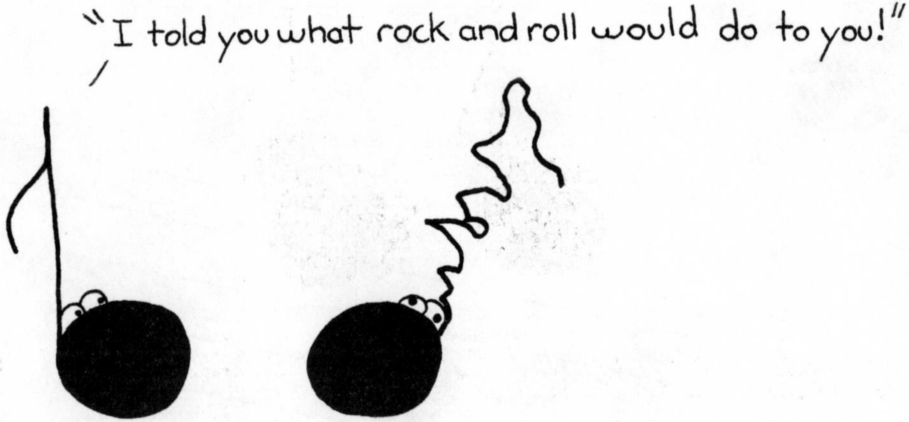
"I told you what rock and roll would do to you!"

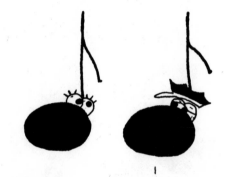

"Can't you read the signs lady?, You're doing 45 in a 33⅓ zone!"

"when I said I wanted a <u>hit man</u>, I meant a songwriter."

"Give up Bugsy! It's time you face the music!"

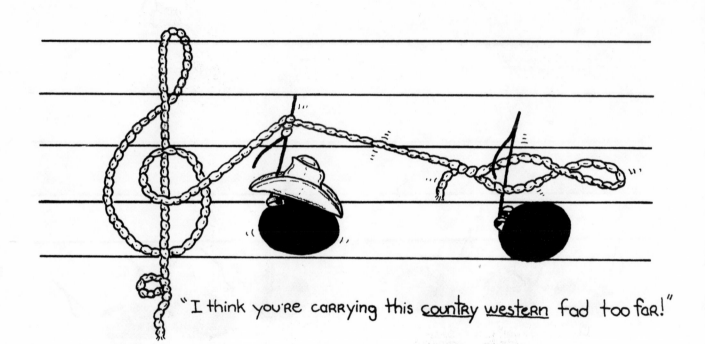

"Remember, keep an eye out for ticket scalpers."

"I thought you said this concert was reserved seating."

"That, my friend, was the loan <u>arranger!</u>"

"Now there's a woman with a <u>classic</u> bust!"

"I hate <u>canned</u> music."

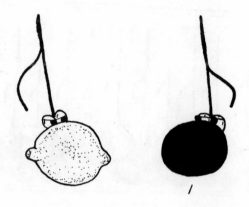

"with such a sour attitude you won't get far!"

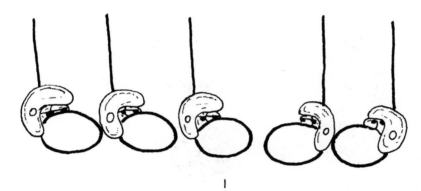

"Now remember, the object is to get their quarterback"

"I certainly hope that New Wave isn't permanent."

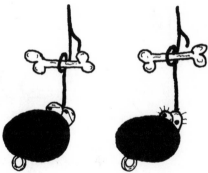

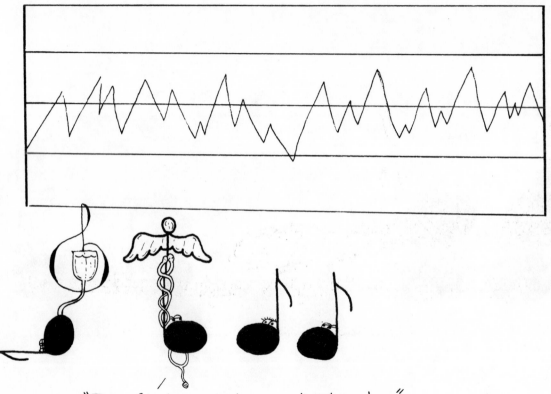

"I'm afraid your son has overdosed on disco."

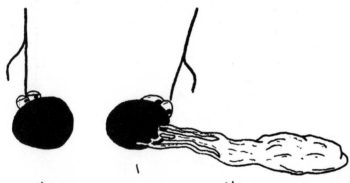

"There's nothing worse than getting caught up in bubble gum music."

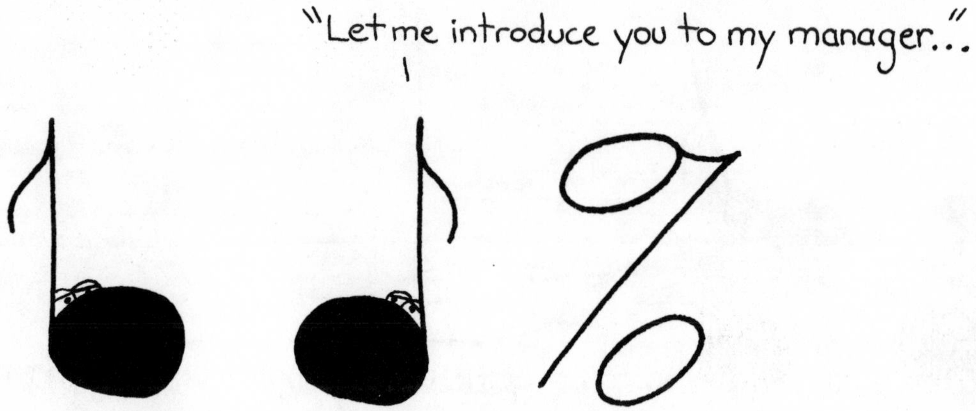
"Let me introduce you to my manager..."

"My recipe for a hit song?... A simple tune, catchy lyrics and a brother who owns a record company."

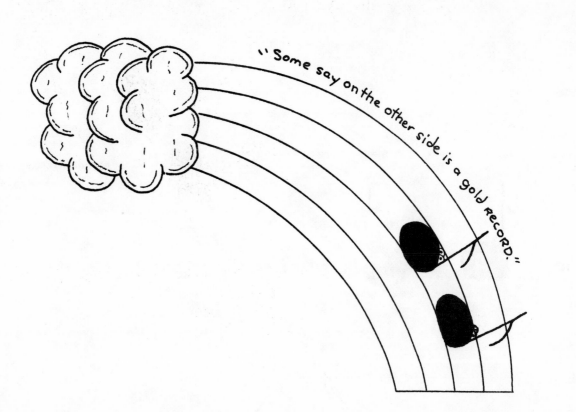

"It's not easy getting a hit record; you have to climb the charts!"

"Timbre!!!"

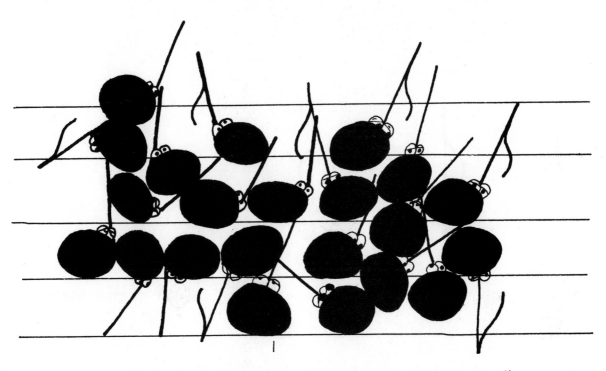

"I wish these <u>jam</u> sessions were a little more orchestrated."

"I don't mind cutting albums, I just don't want to get stuck in the same old <u>groove</u>."

"Frankly I'm a little worried about these staff cutbacks."

"Remember brothers and sisters we've got to live together in harmony!"

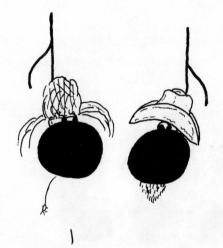

"Sure I like bluegrass musicians, I just wish they weren't so picky!"

"I'm sick of his <u>wholier</u> than thou attitude."

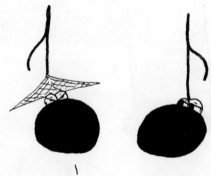

"The trouble with rock and roll is it all sounds alike!"

"Look..., a couple of old timers from the swing era."

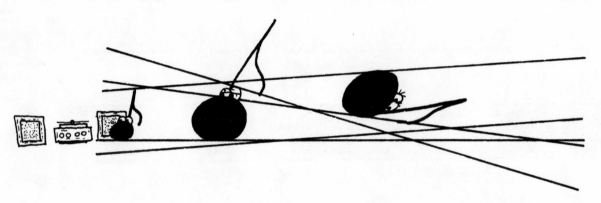

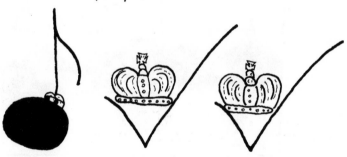

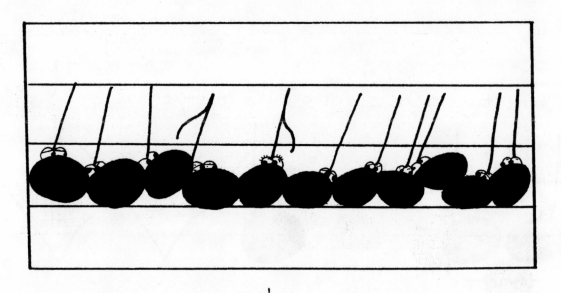

"Darling, I'm tired of living in these cramped quarters."

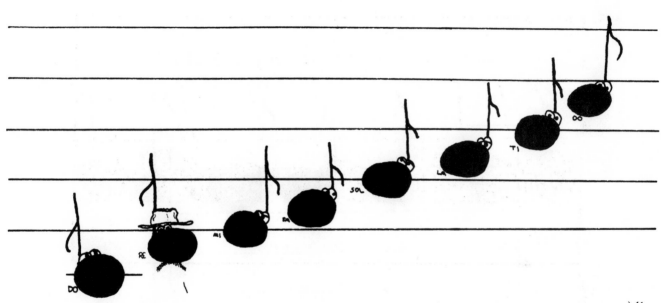

"Now you can call me <u>RE</u>, or you can call me Raymond, or you can . . ."

A Short Biography of Rubes®

Rubes was an elementary school dropout; however, he did play a mean kazoo.

After bumming around for about twenty years he decided to educate himself and enrolled in the University of Hard Knocks, where he majored in the fine arts (or not so fine arts, as the case may be).

Determined not to become another starving musician, he mastered pots and pans, trash can lids and the comb and tissue.

Wishing to share his talents with the world, he has published his musical works and has made them readily available to the public.

Shunning the limelight (and arrest for disturbing the peace), he currently uses the stage name "Leigh."

Rubes is currently touring the U.S., where he performs only the most popular street corners, parks, and alleys.